LEDGER BOOK

Name: _____

Phone: _____

D1122669

Year: _____

No.	Date	Description	Account	Income	Expenses	Total

Year: _____

No.	Date	Description	Account	Income	Expenses	Total

Year: _____

No.	Date	Description	Account	Income	Expenses	Total

Year: _____

No.	Date	Description	Account	Income	Expenses	Total

Year: _____

No.	Date	Description	Account	Income	Expenses	Total

Year: _____

No.	Date	Description	Account	Income	Expenses	Total

Year: _____

No.	Date	Description	Account	Income	Expenses	Total

Year: _____

No.	Date	Description	Account	Income	Expenses	Total

Year: _____

No.	Date	Description	Account	Income	Expenses	Total

Year: _____

No.	Date	Description	Account	Income	Expenses	Total

Year: _____

No.	Date	Description	Account	Income	Expenses	Total

Year: _____

No.	Date	Description	Account	Income	Expenses	Total

Year: _____

No.	Date	Description	Account	Income	Expenses	Total

Year: _____

No.	Date	Description	Account	Income	Expenses	Total

Year: _____

No.	Date	Description	Account	Income	Expenses	Total

Year: _____

No.	Date	Description	Account	Income	Expenses	Total

Year: _____

No.	Date	Description	Account	Income	Expenses	Total

Year: _____

No.	Date	Description	Account	Income	Expenses	Total

Year: _____

No.	Date	Description	Account	Income	Expenses	Total

Year: _____

No.	Date	Description	Account	Income	Expenses	Total

Year: _____

No.	Date	Description	Account	Income	Expenses	Total

Year: _____

No.	Date	Description	Account	Income	Expenses	Total

Year: _____

No.	Date	Description	Account	Income	Expenses	Total

Year: _____

No.	Date	Description	Account	Income	Expenses	Total

Year: _____

No.	Date	Description	Account	Income	Expenses	Total

Year: _____

No.	Date	Description	Account	Income	Expenses	Total

Year: _____

No.	Date	Description	Account	Income	Expenses	Total

Year: _____

No.	Date	Description	Account	Income	Expenses	Total

Year: _____

No.	Date	Description	Account	Income	Expenses	Total

Year: _____

No.	Date	Description	Account	Income	Expenses	Total

Year: _____

No.	Date	Description	Account	Income	Expenses	Total

Year: _____

No.	Date	Description	Account	Income	Expenses	Total

Year: _____

No.	Date	Description	Account	Income	Expenses	Total

Year: _____

No.	Date	Description	Account	Income	Expenses	Total

Year: _____

No.	Date	Description	Account	Income	Expenses	Total

Year: _____

No.	Date	Description	Account	Income	Expenses	Total

Year: _____

No.	Date	Description	Account	Income	Expenses	Total

Year: _____

No.	Date	Description	Account	Income	Expenses	Total

Year: _____

No.	Date	Description	Account	Income	Expenses	Total

Year: _____

No.	Date	Description	Account	Income	Expenses	Total

Year: _____

No.	Date	Description	Account	Income	Expenses	Total

Year: _____

No.	Date	Description	Account	Income	Expenses	Total

Year: _____

No.	Date	Description	Account	Income	Expenses	Total

Year: _____

No.	Date	Description	Account	Income	Expenses	Total

Year: _____

No.	Date	Description	Account	Income	Expenses	Total

Year: _____

No.	Date	Description	Account	Income	Expenses	Total

Year: _____

No.	Date	Description	Account	Income	Expenses	Total

Year: _____

No.	Date	Description	Account	Income	Expenses	Total

Year: _____

No.	Date	Description	Account	Income	Expenses	Total

Year: _____

No.	Date	Description	Account	Income	Expenses	Total

Year: _____

No.	Date	Description	Account	Income	Expenses	Total

Year: _____

No.	Date	Description	Account	Income	Expenses	Total

Year: _____

No.	Date	Description	Account	Income	Expenses	Total

Year: _____

No.	Date	Description	Account	Income	Expenses	Total

Year: _____

No.	Date	Description	Account	Income	Expenses	Total

Year: _____

No.	Date	Description	Account	Income	Expenses	Total

Year: _____

No.	Date	Description	Account	Income	Expenses	Total

Year: _____

No.	Date	Description	Account	Income	Expenses	Total

Year: _____

No.	Date	Description	Account	Income	Expenses	Total

Year: _____

No.	Date	Description	Account	Income	Expenses	Total

Year: _____

No.	Date	Description	Account	Income	Expenses	Total

Year: _____

No.	Date	Description	Account	Income	Expenses	Total

Year: _____

No.	Date	Description	Account	Income	Expenses	Total

Year: _____

No.	Date	Description	Account	Income	Expenses	Total

Year: _____

No.	Date	Description	Account	Income	Expenses	Total

Year: _____

No.	Date	Description	Account	Income	Expenses	Total

Year: _____

No.	Date	Description	Account	Income	Expenses	Total

Year: _____

No.	Date	Description	Account	Income	Expenses	Total

Year: _____

No.	Date	Description	Account	Income	Expenses	Total

Year: _____

No.	Date	Description	Account	Income	Expenses	Total

Year: _____

No.	Date	Description	Account	Income	Expenses	Total

Year: _____

No.	Date	Description	Account	Income	Expenses	Total

Year: _____

No.	Date	Description	Account	Income	Expenses	Total

Year: _____

No.	Date	Description	Account	Income	Expenses	Total

Year: _____

No.	Date	Description	Account	Income	Expenses	Total

Year: _____

No.	Date	Description	Account	Income	Expenses	Total

Year: _____

No.	Date	Description	Account	Income	Expenses	Total

Year: _____

No.	Date	Description	Account	Income	Expenses	Total

Year: _____

No.	Date	Description	Account	Income	Expenses	Total

Year: _____

No.	Date	Description	Account	Income	Expenses	Total

Year: _____

No.	Date	Description	Account	Income	Expenses	Total

Year: _____

No.	Date	Description	Account	Income	Expenses	Total

Year: _____

No.	Date	Description	Account	Income	Expenses	Total

Year: _____

No.	Date	Description	Account	Income	Expenses	Total

Year: _____

No.	Date	Description	Account	Income	Expenses	Total

Year: _____

No.	Date	Description	Account	Income	Expenses	Total

Year: _____

No.	Date	Description	Account	Income	Expenses	Total

Year: _____

No.	Date	Description	Account	Income	Expenses	Total

Year: _____

No.	Date	Description	Account	Income	Expenses	Total

Year: _____

No.	Date	Description	Account	Income	Expenses	Total

Year: _____

No.	Date	Description	Account	Income	Expenses	Total

Year: _____

No.	Date	Description	Account	Income	Expenses	Total

Year: _____

No.	Date	Description	Account	Income	Expenses	Total

Year: _____

No.	Date	Description	Account	Income	Expenses	Total

Year: _____

No.	Date	Description	Account	Income	Expenses	Total

Year: _____

No.	Date	Description	Account	Income	Expenses	Total

Year: _____

No.	Date	Description	Account	Income	Expenses	Total

Year: _____

No.	Date	Description	Account	Income	Expenses	Total

Year: _____

No.	Date	Description	Account	Income	Expenses	Total

Year: _____

No.	Date	Description	Account	Income	Expenses	Total

Year: _____

No.	Date	Description	Account	Income	Expenses	Total

Year: _____

No.	Date	Description	Account	Income	Expenses	Total

Year: _____

No.	Date	Description	Account	Income	Expenses	Total

Year: _____

No.	Date	Description	Account	Income	Expenses	Total

Year: _____

No.	Date	Description	Account	Income	Expenses	Total

Year: _____

No.	Date	Description	Account	Income	Expenses	Total

Year: _____

No.	Date	Description	Account	Income	Expenses	Total

Year: _____

No.	Date	Description	Account	Income	Expenses	Total

Year: _____

No.	Date	Description	Account	Income	Expenses	Total

Year: _____

No.	Date	Description	Account	Income	Expenses	Total